Why did Garfield take a nap in the fireplace?

> He wanted to sleep like a log.

Why did the dog cross the road?

> To slobber on the other side.

What's the first thing Garfield loses when he's on a diet?

> His sense of humor.

Also by Jim Davis:
Published by Ballantine Books:

GARFIELD'S BIG FAT HAIRY JOKE BOOK

Created by
Jim Davis

Written by
Jim Kraft and Mark Acey

BALLANTINE BOOKS • NEW YORK

Copyright © 1994 United Feature Syndicate, Inc.

All rights reserved under International and Pan-American Copyright Conventions. Published in the United States of America by Ballantine Books, a division of Random House, Inc., New York, and simultaneously in Canada by Random House of Canada Limited, Toronto.

Library of Congress Catalog Card Number: 93-90706

ISBN 0-345-38640-X

Manufactured in the United States of America

First Edition: February 1994

CONTENTS

GOING TO THE DOGS

*Life's a bowl of cherries,
and dogs are the pits*

What do you call the black spot between a dog's ears?
The hole where its brain should be.

What's the difference between a barking dog and an
    umbrella?
You can shut the umbrella up!

How can you tell when you have a slow dog?
He brings you yesterday's newspaper.

"What's your dog's name?"
"Melonhead."
"That's a pretty stupid name."
"He's a pretty stupid dog."

Don't go out if it's raining cats and dogs. You might
    step in a poodle!

3

Why did the watchdog keep turning in circles?
He was winding himself up!

What kind of dog washes clothes?
A laundromutt!

How can you tell if your dog's been drinking from the
toilet?
His breath smells better.

Why does Garfield like big dogs?
He doesn't have to bend down to pull their tails.

What would you get if you crossed a frog with a dog?
A croaker spaniel.

Why is a dog like a tree?
They both have a lot of bark.

There once was a dog who didn't have a nose. Do you
know how he smelled?
Awful!

What would you get if you crossed a dog with an elephant?
A squashed dog!

What is Garfield's favorite type of dog?
A hot dog!

How many dogs does it take to make a fur coat?
None. Dogs can't sew!

What kind of fish do dogs prefer?
Catfish!

What's noisy, smelly, and has an I.Q. of 12?
A dozen dogs!

What's green, flea-bitten, and slobbers on Tokyo?
Dogzilla.

What would you call a meeting of dogs?
A bow-wow pow-wow.

Why did the old dog's bones ache?
He had arfritis!

What would you get if you crossed a dog with a
    nine-foot gorilla?
A gorilla who drinks out of any toilet he pleases!

What should you give a carsick dog?
Bus fare!

Why did God create dogs?
So warthogs would have something to laugh at.

What kind of dog says "meow"?
An undercover police dog.

What do you call a smart dog?
A freak of nature!

What kind of dog would make a good pilot?
An Airedale.

What's uglier and dumber than a dog?
Two dogs!

What do you give a dog with a fever?
Mustard. It's the best thing for a hot dog!

Why are dogs like nails?
They both need a good whack on the head!

Where do people leave their dogs when they go
shopping?
In the barking lot.

What do you have to know to teach a dog tricks?
More than the dog.

Dogs are smarter than they look. But then, they'd
have to be!

Why are dogs like hamburger?
They're both sold by the pound.

7

Did you hear about the dog who could cook breakfast?
His specialty was pooched eggs.

Why did the dog cross the road?
To slobber on the other side.

What's black and white and red all over?
A Dalmatian with a sunburn!

What kind of dog would make a good deli snack?
A beagle with cream cheese!

Did you hear about the dog who married a fish?
They had a litter of guppies!

Knock knock!
Who's there?
Fido.
Fido who?
Fido know. . . . I'm just a dumb dog!

Did you hear about the dog all of the other dogs avoided?
Seems he had a bad case of "peoplebreath."

How did the bulldog burn his nose?
He tried to iron the wrinkles out of his face.

"My dog can jump higher than my house!"
"No, he can't!"
"Sure he can. My house can't jump!"

How should you talk to a big, angry dog?
From as far away as possible!

"I'm having trouble training my dog."
"Maybe you should get a dog-training book."
"Why? My dog can't read."

What's the difference between a dog and a stick?
One is an inanimate object that clutters up the lawn, and the other is a piece of wood.

How many dogs does it take to replace a light bulb?
One ... but you have to screw him in real tight!

Cats are poetry in motion. Dogs are gibberish in
  neutral.

Higher life forms always evolve from lower ones.
Which must mean that rocks evolved from dogs.

TOP TEN REASONS DOGS ARE
EXPELLED FROM OBEDIENCE SCHOOL

10. Drinking from faculty toilet
 9. Never turning in homework. Always claiming
     owner ate it
 8. Licking themselves during the Pledge of Alle-
     giance
 7. Violating school dress code with "Cats Suck"
     T-shirt
 6. Carjacking
 5. Playing hooky when they should be playing dead
 4. Cutting line at the hydrant
 3. Continuous barking during study hall
 2. Hiding crib notes on back of flea collar
 1. Gnawing on trainer

WELCOME TO THE FUNNY FARM

*It doesn't get
any cornier than this!*

Did you hear about the cow who couldn't give milk?
She was an udder failure!

What do you call an egg who thinks of nothing but
    himself?
An eggomaniac.

Why was the baby horse shivering?
Because he was a little colt.

Did you hear about the farmer whose buildings kept
    disappearing?
Guess he was just a barn loser!

What has feathers, webbed feet, and rows of razor-sharp
    teeth?
A Great White Duck.

Why did the farmer take a baseball bat out to the
    barn?
His wife said it was time to hit the hay!

Why did the pig say "Cock-a-doodle-doo"?
Because it was the rooster's day off.

Why is a man with a sore throat like a pony?
They're both a little ho(a)rse.

What's the best way to keep a bull from charging?
Take away his credit cards!

What does a farmer use to count his cows?
A cowculator!

Shepherd: "I'll watch your sheep, but I won't herd
    them back to the barn."
Farmer: "Why not?"
Shepherd: "Sheep should be seen, and not herded."

Why did the farmer jiggle the cow?
He was trying to make a milkshake!

What's the difference between pig slop and Garfield?
One is hog food and the other's a food hog!

"My ox ran into my tractor."
"Did he do it on purpose?"
"No, it was an oxident."

"It certainly was hot on the farm last week."
"How hot was it?"
"It was so hot, the chickens were laying hard-boiled
    eggs!"

If people eat chicken noodle soup, do chickens eat
    people noodle soup?

"I have a piglet named 'Ink.'"
"Why do you call him 'Ink'?"
"Because he's always running out of the pen!"

Jon: "These same ducks have lived on our farm for
    many years."
Garfield: "Maybe it's time to reduckorate!"

15

Why did Odie try to ride the mean horse?
Garfield told him it was a way to get big bucks!

Why do chickens eat bugs?
Because they're too dumb to order pizza!

Why did the boy throw the chicken through the basketball hoop?
He was practicing his fowl shot!

How did Garfield stop the rooster from waking him on Monday morning?
He ate him for dinner Sunday night!

If a little pig is a piglet, what do you call a little chicken?
An omelet!

What's the best way to call a hog?
Get his number and dial direct.

What does a flock of tough sheep say?
"We're baaaa-d!"

What do farmers give their wives on Valentine's Day?
Hogs and kisses!

What is a duck's favorite breakfast cereal?
Quacker Oats!

"I think goats are very rude animals."
"Why is that?"
"They're always butting in!"

"My duck is sick. What should I do?"
"Call a ducktor!"

How does a chicken change a light bulb?
She doesn't. She just thinks she's gone blind.

What did one cornstalk say to the other?
"I'm all ears!"

What animal goes "Gobble, gobble, gobble"?
Garfield at the dinner table!

Why didn't Garfield wake Jon's brother?
Because you should always let sleeping Docs lie.

What happened to the duck who worried too much?
He quacked up!

Where would you find famous paintings by cows?
In an art moo-seum!

When is a hot air balloon like a place to store hay?
When it's aloft.

Why did the farmer put aspirin in his fields and house
    windows?
Because he heard it was good for acres and panes!

What state has the most cows?
Moo Jersey.

"Why are you feeding nails to your goat?"
"Because the vet said he should eat more iron."

Teacher: "Who was the thirteenth president of the United States?"
Student: "A duck."
Teacher: "A duck?"
Student: "Yep. *Mallard* Fillmore!"

Did you hear about the farmer who fed crayons to his chickens?
He wanted them to lay colored eggs!

Did you hear about the pig who went into show business?
He loved to ham it up!

At daybreak the rooster hopped onto Farmer Willard's bedroom windowsill and began to crow. Farmer Willard picked up a shoe and hurled it at the rooster, knocking the bird to the ground. Five minutes later the rooster climbed back onto the windowsill and began crowing again. Again Farmer Willard hurled a shoe, knocking the poor rooster to the ground. Five minutes later, the same thing happened. Annoyed, the farmer's sleepy wife grumbled, "Willard, I don't care whether you get up or not. But I wish you'd stop hitting the snooze alarm!"

Did you hear about the hen who got caught in the tornado?
After that she laid nothing but scrambled eggs!

GARFIELD'S TOP TEN FAVORITE THINGS TO DO ON THE ARBUCKLE FARM

10. Put down Roy Clark and the whole "Hee Haw" gang
 9. Shake up the animals with some frank talk about the food chain
 8. Give Odie a good threshing
 7. Plant some chickens
 6. Fertilize Doc Boy's overalls
 5. Baste the hogs
 4. Party till the cows come home, then party with the cows
 3. Hit the hay
 2. Harvest the fridge
 1. Leave

THAT'S GARFIELD!

*I'm not overweight,
I'm undertall*

Why is Garfield like a leaky bathtub?
You can never fill him up!

Garfield is so fat, Jon exercises by running laps
around him!

What follows Garfield wherever he goes?
His tail.

Why did Garfield take a ruler to bed?
To see how long he slept.

Who is Garfield's favorite movie star?
The Blob. Garfield likes anything that can eat a whole
town!

What did Garfield say to the fleas?
"Don't bug me!"

Why did Garfield take a bath after stealing Odie's
    dinner?
He wanted to make a clean getaway.

If you dropped Garfield into a bowl of punch, what
    would you get?
Out of there as fast as you can!

What's the only bird that can lift Garfield?
A crane.

Why is Garfield like one of the Great Lakes?
Because he's so Superior!

Who is Garfield's favorite historical figure?
Nap-oleon.

Which side of Garfield has the most fur?
The outside!

What is Garfield's favorite state?
A state of unconsciousness.

Why did Garfield go to the dog pound?
He wanted to pound the dogs!

What is Garfield's favorite day of the week?
Friesday.

Why is Garfield like a secret agent?
He's usually under cover!

Is Garfield afraid of man-eating sharks?
No, he's afraid of cat-eating sharks.

What is Garfield's favorite time to eat?
Anytime!

What is Garfield's favorite thing to put in a pie?
His teeth.

What's the only fast thing that Garfield can catch?
Fast food!

Is Garfield a light sleeper?
Yes, but he'd rather sleep in the dark.

The only thing active about Garfield is his imagination!

What's the difference between Garfield and a sofa?
If you have to, you can lift a sofa.

Why is Garfield like a flower?
He's usually found in a bed.

Garfield is so fat, the phone company gave him his
own area code!

What is Garfield's favorite type of story?
A furry tale.

Why does Garfield attack the mailman?
He doesn't think dogs should have all the fun!

Garfield is so slow, he can't even catch a cold!

What is Garfield's favorite mountain?
Mt. Ever-rest!

Garfield went on a fourteen-day diet. Do you know
    what he lost?
Two weeks!

When is Garfield like a piece of wood?
When he's bored.

How would Garfield look in a ballet costume?
Tutu fat!

What's the first thing Garfield loses when he's on a
    diet?
His sense of humor.

Why is Garfield like a comet?
They're both stars that have tails.

What is Garfield's favorite bird?
A swallow.

Garfield is so fat, a NASA satellite once went into orbit
around him!

Garfield always watches what he eats. Otherwise some
crumbs might get away!

Garfield was sick, so he went to the vet. And now he's
feline fine!

How can you tell Garfield from an easy chair?
The easy chair has a lot less padding!

Why was Garfield hissing at the tree?
Because it was a dogwood.

How many meals does Garfield eat each day?
As many as he can get!

Why did Garfield turn off the TV?
It wasn't insulting his intelligence.

Garfield is so fat, when he rolls over, it registers on
the Richter scale!

Why does Garfield spend so much time sleeping?
Because he can.

What does Garfield get after he eats way too much
lasagna?
Dessert, of course!

What is Garfield's favorite type of car?
A Cat-illac.

Garfield's idea of exercise is a brisk two-hour nap!

Garfield is so lazy, he hired someone to breathe for him!

How is the Grand Canyon different from Garfield's stomach?
The Grand Canyon isn't bottomless.

What would you get if you crossed Garfield with a canary?
One less canary.

Why did Garfield put insect spray on Jon's watch?
Because it was full of ticks.

Garfield is so fat, someone once tried to climb his north slope.

Garfield doesn't spend his whole day lying in bed. He also lies on the couch!

I'm not saying that Garfield eats constantly, but he has the only refrigerator with a pet door!

GARFIELD'S TOP TEN
FAVORITE WAYS TO SLEEP

10. Late
 9. Deep
 8. Holding his Pooky
 7. Like the dead
 6. Deader than that
 5. Like Rip van Winkle on Sominex
 4. Lying down
 3. Like a log in a coma
 2. On a full stomach
 1. Constantly

SPORTS
SHORTS

Spitball? What Spitball?

What did the baseball glove say to the baseball?
"Catch you later!"

When is a hockey player like a magician?
When he does a hat trick.

What would you get if you crossed a ghost with a
famous two-sport athlete?
Boo Jackson!

What happens if you hit a yellow golf ball into the Red
Sea?
It gets wet.

What ball does Garfield most like to catch?
A meatball!

How does Michael Jordan change a light bulb?
He fakes it out of its socket.

What football position is Garfield most likely to play?
Wide receiver.

What do you call it when Odie hits a hockey puck with
his tongue?
A slurp shot!

Why do hockey players wear padded gloves?
So they can save their fists for hockey fights.

What would you get if you crossed a famous boxer
with a bowling lane?
Muhammad Alley.

What did the cup say to the golf ball?
"Drop in any time."

How is Garfield like a basketball?
They're both round, orange, and frequently stuffed!

Why did the pitcher take a blanket onto the baseball field?
In case he had to cover first base.

Why do hockey players wear helmets?
In case they bump heads as they're picking up their teeth.

What did the bowling ball say to the bowling pins?
"Don't stop me. I'm on a roll!"

What's the difference between broccoli and a basketball?
If you had to, you could eat a basketball.

How does Dan Marino change a light bulb?
He passes the job to a receiver.

What was that stain on the hockey player's uniform?
Rink around the collar.

Knock knock!
Who's there?
Randy.
Randy who?
Randy marathon . . . and boy, am I pooped!

What would you get if you crossed a Swedish tennis
     star with a breakfast cereal?
Bjorn Flakes!

Why is a stuffed Dracula like three balls and two
     strikes?
They're both full counts!

Why were the police staking out the baseball field?
They heard the players were stealing bases.

When Garfield went golfing, he got two birdies and an
     eagle. But he was still hungry!

"I've been swimming since I was five years old."
"Gosh, you must be exhausted!"

What professional baseball team is the scariest?
The Toronto Boo Jays.

Did you hear about the pole vaulter who was having a
    bad day?
His vaults weren't quite up to bar.

How did the tennis player feel when he hit a good
    shot?
Volley happy.

"My ankle is too sore to jog today."
"Now that's a lame excuse!"

How does Nolan Ryan change a lightbulb?
Three twists and it's out!

How did the lousy golfer reduce his score by 120
    strokes?
He stopped playing golf!

"When I play golf, I always shoot in the eighties."
"Really?"
"Yes, if it gets any hotter than that, I don't play."

Why is it hard to nap during a tennis match?
Because of all the racquet!

What do you call it when a pig hits a baseball out of the park?
A ham run!

Then there was the golfer whose drives went like lightning. In other words, they usually hit a tree!

What's the hardest thing about playing water polo?
Finding a horse that can swim!

Why did the hockey player bring chocolate frosting to the rink?
In case he needed to ice the puck!

Why did the surfer cross the ocean?
To get to the other tide.

"Are you a serious soccer player?"
"No, I just play for kicks."

Why did the hurried bowler want to roll a strike?
Because he had no time to spare!

What kind of dog would make a good baseball player?
A Doberman Pitcher.

How does a professional tennis player change a light
bulb?
He screams until the umpire changes it for him.

Why is a jeweler like a baseball player?
They both spend a lot of time on diamonds.

What famous building is named after a baseball official?
The Umpire State Building.

Why did the man tell his date that he was a hockey
    player?
So she'd think he was an ice guy.

What would you get if you crossed a famous hockey
    player with a popular Southern food?
Wayne Gritsky!

Why was it so breezy in the football stadium?
Because it was full of fans.

Why is it so hard to drive a golf ball?
Because it doesn't have a steering wheel.

Why did the golfer wear two pairs of pants?
In case he got a hole in one.

TOP TEN REASONS
GARFIELD CAN'T PLAY IN THE NBA

10. Hates being cooped up in pet carrier during road
    trips
 9. Tough to rebound with guys standing on your tail
 8. Goes to sleep on defense ... literally

7. Shoots too many hairballs
6. Astronomical wage demands would push teams over salary cap
5. Major girth precludes serious hangtime
4. One whiff of locker room, he loses his lunch
3. Notorious trash talker. Can't back it up
2. His only moves are toward concession stand
1. For Pete's sake, he's a cat!

HOT AND COLD RUNNING GAGS

Call my school.
Tell them I died

Why did the boy take a baseball glove to the pool?
He wanted to catch some rays!

What happens when the sun gets tired?
It sets for a while.

Knock knock!
Who's there?
Gladys.
Gladys who?
Gladys summer! Aren't you?

What's orange, furry, and has a trunk?
Garfield going on vacation!

What kind of bath can you take without water?
A sun bath.

What has four legs and flies?
A picnic table.

Jon: "Let's take a dip in the ocean."
Garfield: "I'll take Odie. Who will you take?"

Why did the man take light bulbs to the beach?
In case he wanted a light snack!

What did the ocean say to the girl?
Nothing. It only waved.

Why is Garfield at the beach like Christmas?
They both have sandy claws!

Knock knock!
Who's there?
Rob.
Rob who?
Rob some sunblock on me before I burn up!

"My dad has a car phone."
"Big deal. My dad has a carpool!"

What would you get if you crossed two fish with two
    elephants?
A pair of swimming trunks!

What happened when the beach met the ocean?
The ocean made him shore!

"It was really hot at the zoo yesterday."
"How hot was it?"
"It was so hot, the penguins were wearing Bermuda
    shorts."

Teacher: "What's the most dangerous animal in the
    desert?"
Student: "The polar bear."
Teacher: "The polar bear? But a polar bear lives at the
    North Pole."
Student: "Right. So if he woke up in the desert, he'd
    be mad as heck!"

What did the lizard say to the cactus?
"I see your point."

Student: "Someday I'll fly on a rocket to the sun!"
Teacher: "But the sun's so hot, you'll burn up!"
Student: "That's why I'm going at night."

Tourist: "How long should I stay out in the sun?"
Hotel Clerk: "You'll have to ask the chef."
Tourist: "The chef?"
Hotel Clerk: "Yes. He handles all the baking."

What did the tourist say to the Statue of Liberty?
"Keep in torch!"

What's cold, white, and falls up?
A snowflake with no sense of direction.

Where do Eskimos keep their money?
In snowbanks!

Why did Garfield throw Nermal into the snow?
He wanted Nermal to chill out!

What's the difference between a snowman and Odie?
One has snow brains and the other has no brains!

What kind of dogs should you wear on your head in
    winter?
Earmutts.

Why is a snowstorm like the Arbuckle family?
They both have lots of flakes.

Why do birds fly south for the winter?
Because it's faster than taking a bus!

Why should you wait until winter to buy a thermometer?
Because they're lower in winter.

What do fleas do in the winter?
They fleeze!

What is Frosty's favorite dinner?
Spaghetti and snowballs.

When is lunch like winter weather?
When it's chili.

"Do you jog during the winter?"
"No, but sometimes my nose runs!"

What would you call a frozen Odie?
A pupsicle!

Why did the man wear galoshes to bed?
In case he had sleet dreams.

What's big, ugly, and drools on the mountains?
The Abominable Snowdog.

What do you call Pooky when he's on a toboggan?
A sleddy bear.

What type of exercises do penguins do?
Ice-ometrics.

Why did the woman ski down Mt. McKinley?
Because it was easier than skiing up!

How do you make a sled slow down?
Give it a sledative.

Why is Jon's mind like snow?
It tends to drift.

Why did Garfield take a nap in the fireplace?
He wanted to sleep like a log!

In winter, what falls but never hits the ground?
The temperature.

Then there was the woman who was so fashion-conscious
that when she went out in a blizzard, she wore high-
heeled snowshoes.

Why is the Arctic Ocean so cold?
Because it's wearing an ice cap.

What would you call Jon's toboggan?
A boobsled.

What do Odie's brain and the Abominable Snowman
   have in common?
Neither one has ever been found!

GARFIELD'S TOP TEN
SIGNS OF SPRING

10. Pizza delivery guy no longer using dogsled
 9. Last needle falls off Jon's Christmas tree
 8. Drool-sicle on Odie's chin begins to melt
 7. Birds at bird feeder show off Florida tans
 6. Nights get—ugh!—shorter
 5. Jon stops wearing pajamas with feet
 4. Ground turns a lovely shade of mud
 3. First robin slams into your picture window
 2. Oh, yeah—new leaves
 1. Frosty starts sweating bullets

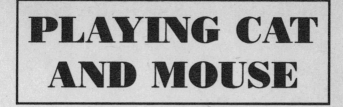

PLAYING CAT AND MOUSE

*Show me a good mouser,
and I'll show you a cat
with bad breath*

Why do cats nap so much?
So they'll be rested when it's time for bed.

What do cats have that no other animals have?
Kittens!

Why do mice live in the walls?
Because they can't afford the whole apartment!

What Russian city has the most mice?
Mouscow.

Why did Garfield ask Odie to help him chase the
    mice?
Because mousery loves company.

What has big ears, a long tail, and is crowned in Atlantic
    City?
Mouse America.

What is a cat's favorite breakfast cereal?
Mice Krispies.

What did Garfield say after Squeak ate all the cheese?
Nothing. He knows you shouldn't talk when your
    mouth is full.

Can Garfield catch a mouse?
Yes, if someone throws one at him!

Which is smarter, a cat or a chicken?
Well, have you ever seen "Kentucky Fried Cat"?

What does a 300-lb. mouse say?
"Here, kitty, kitty, kitty!"

What kind of cat should you never play games with?
A cheetah.

What would you get if you crossed a cat with a
    computer?
A machine that scratches and bytes!

What do cats put in their drinks to keep them cold?
Mice cubes!

What kind of mouse is even fatter than Garfield?
A hippopotamouse!

How do you make a cat float?
Two scoops of ice cream, some root beer, and a cat!

When is Garfield not a cat?
When he walks down the street and turns into a res-
    taurant.

What kind of kitten can fix a cut?
A first-aid kit-ten.

What three letters turn a kitten into a cat?
A-G-E.

59

What do all cats like to be called?
They like to be called for dinner.

Can cats see in the dark?
Yes, but they have trouble holding the flashlight!

Where's the best place to bury a mouse?
In a mouse-oleum.

Why do cats make the best pets?
Because they're purrfect!

Where's the best place to find a gift for a cat?
In a cat-alog.

How can you tell if a cat burglar has been in your
    house?
Your cat is missing!

"I can spell 'mousetrap' with just three letters."
"How can you do that?"
"Easy. 'C-A-T.' "

What do cats use to get rid of that mouse aftertaste?
Mousewash.

Did you hear about the female cat who swallowed a
    ball of yarn?
She had mittens!

What do you call a cat who cuts your grass?
A lawn meower.

What did the cat say when he met the mouse?
"Pleased to eat you."

What has antlers and runs around Walt Disney World?
Mickey Moose!

What is a mouse's favorite dessert?
Cheesecake!

"My cat plays the piano."
"Really. Does he play by ear?"
"No, he uses his paws."

If Leonardo da Vinci had been a mouse, would the "Mona Lisa" be considered a mouseterpiece?

Why do cats have nine lives?
So they can cross the street eight times without looking.

What famous river is named after a mouse?
The Moussissippi.

How are cats like bottles of fine wine?
They mostly lie around getting dusty.

What would you get if you crossed a mouse with a duck?
A mouse that likes cheese and quackers!

What would you call Squeak's wife?
A mouse spouse.

What is a cat's favorite dessert?
Mice pudding!

"I just got a new collar for my cat."
"Wish I could make a trade like that."

Customer: "These mousetraps you sold me don't work."
Clerk: "Did you bait them?"
Customer: "With my own hands."
Clerk: "Well, next time try using cheese."

What has twelve legs, three tails, and swashbuckles?
The Three Mouseketeers.

Why do cats chase mice?
Because it would look silly if the mice chased them.

If a mouse lost its tail, where would it get a new one?
At a re-tail store.

GARFIELD'S TOP TEN EXCUSES FOR NOT CATCHING A MOUSE

10. "I thought it was just a squeaky dustball"
 9. "I tore a rotator cuff"
 8. "The mouse had a restraining order"

7. "I left my instincts in another life"
6. "Gandhi made me not do it"
5. "I come from a lazy home"
4. "Jon's cooking kills them faster"
3. "You mean mice *aren't* an endangered species?"
2. "I'm on a no-vermin diet"
1. "Basically, I don't give a mouse dropping"

NOW WE'RE COOKING!

*Some of my best friends
are calories*

Why did the woman wear a helmet at the dinner table?
She was on a crash diet.

What did the boy say to the lollipop?
"I can lick you any day!"

How is Garfield like a lousy cook?
His meals always go to waist.

"That new chef is a very mean man."
"Why do you say that?"
"He told me he was going to whip the cream and beat
    the eggs!"

Knock knock.
Who's there?
Anita.
Anita who?
Anita cup of coffee!

Why should you always keep bananas in the shade?
Because they peel.

What would you get if you crossed a lemon with a cat?
A sourpuss!

What's the difference between a refrigerator and
    Garfield?
One keeps eats and the other keeps eating!

What would Nermal be if he ate Garfield's dinner?
He'd be history!

What did the man get when he accidentally sat on the
    hot stove?
Rump roast!

What are two things you can never eat for lunch?
Breakfast and dinner!

What happened when Garfield met the pan of lasagna?
It was love at first bite!

"Waiter, what is this fly doing in my soup?"
"The backstroke."

"How many cookies can you eat on an empty stomach?"
"I don't know."
"One. After that your stomach isn't empty!"

Knock knock!
Who's there?
Ida.
Ida who?
Ida the lasagna; Garfield's coming!

Did you hear about the clam who didn't have any
     friends?
It's because he was so shellfish.

Why did the man throw lettuce out the window?
His wife asked him to toss the salad.

Why wouldn't the other foods listen to the sandwich?
The sandwich was full of bologna!

Why is Jon's cooking like a volleyball?
You can serve it, but you can't eat it!

"These ribs must have come from the bowling alley."
"What makes you say that?"
"They're *spare* ribs!"

Knock knock!
Who's there?
Olive.
Olive who?
Olive chocolate. Don't you?

What happened when the banana met the ice cream?
The banana split!

The truth is, Garfield only eats two times each day. . . .
Daytime and nighttime!

What's strong, invisible, and smells like lasagna?
Garfield's breath!

"How do you make an apple turnover?"
"I don't know. Try tickling it on one side."

What would you get if you crossed a dog with a
vegetable?
A vegetable that licks your plate clean.

Customer: "What's all that barking in the produce
section?"
Clerk: "We just got a load of collieflower."

Where's the best place to see flying saucers?
A restaurant with clumsy waiters!

"Waiter, my cheesecake is full of holes!"
"Yes, sir. It's Swiss cheesecake."

What would you get if you crossed a dog with a pizza
    topping?
Pupperoni!

"Waiter, what is this antler doing in my dessert?"
"What did you expect, sir? It's chocolate mousse."

What would you call an overcooked sirloin?
A mis-steak!

"Waiter, do you serve fish here?"
"Of course, sir."
"Then bring some bugs for my guppy."

What does a frog get with his hamburger?
A side order of flies.

Did you hear about the new ice cream for monsters?
It's called "Cookies and Scream."

What did one egg say to the other?
"Heard any good yolks lately?"

"Do you eat soup with your right hand or your left?"
"Neither. I use a spoon."

What did the toast say to the knife?
"Stop trying to butter me up!"

What's round, purple, and almost conquered the
    world?
Alexander the Grape.

What kind of peas do the great chefs use?
Reci-peas.

"Waiter, what's the vegetable of the day?"
"It was supposed to be green beans, but someone sat
    on them."
"So what is it now?"
"Squash."

Why did the chef put mouthwash in the soup?
So it wouldn't have bad broth!

"Do you feel like a chocolate sundae?"
"No. Do I look like one?"

Where would you go to mail some lasagna?
To the pasta office!

"Do you know how to make an eggroll?"
"Sure. Just give it a shove."

"Waiter, there's a dead fly in my soup!"
"I'm sorry, sir. We were all out of live ones."

"Waiter, what is the soup of the day?"
"What is today, sir?"
"Tuesday."
"Then it's Tuesday soup."

"Waiter, there's a fly in my soup!"
"I'm sorry, sir. It should be in your salad."

GARFIELD'S TOP TEN
LEAST FAVORITE PASTA DISHES

10. Weaselini
 9. Spaghetti and hairballs
 8. Camelloni
 7. Franco-American "Pasta Pests"
 6. Mousetacholi
 5. Spamicotti
 4. Macaroni and fleas
 3. Fettucine Alberto Styling Mousse
 2. Rigatoenail
 1. Vermincelli

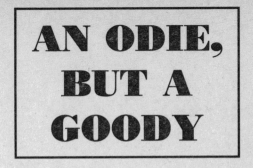

AN ODIE, BUT A GOODY

Take my dog . . . Please!

Odie is so dumb, he thinks a flea market is a place that
sells fleas!

What's the difference between Odie and a nail?
Garfield doesn't need a hammer to pound Odie!

Odie would make a good basketball player. He certainly
knows how to dribble!

What happened when the soda can fell on Odie's foot?
Nothing. It was a soft drink!

What has twenty-one heads, but no brains?
Odie with a book of matches.

What did Garfield do when he found Odie chewing the dictionary?
He took the words right out of his mouth.

Where does Odie sleep when he goes camping?
In a pup tent.

When they were passing out brains, Odie thought they said trains, so he got out of the way!

How do you keep Odie from chewing up the back seat of the car?
Make him sit up front.

Odie is so dumb, he thinks a monkey wrench is something you use to fix a monkey!

What would you get if you crossed Odie with a 500-lb. chicken?
The world's biggest dumb cluck!

What has eight wheels and slobbers?
Odie on roller skates.

Why didn't Odie bark at Garfield?
Because the cat had his tongue!

Odie comes from a military family. His father was a
drool sergeant!

Why did Odie sleep under the leaky old car?
He wanted to get up oily!

Odie is so dumb, he thinks a flower pot is something
you use to cook flowers!

Why does Odie wag his tail?
Because no one will wag it for him!

Odie was bred to be a working dog. Specifically, a
paperweight or a doorstop!

Why is Odie like an empty piggy bank?
Neither of them has any cents!

Why did Garfield tell Odie to stand behind the mule?
He hoped Odie would get a kick out of it!

Odie will never have a mental breakdown. There are
no moving parts up there!

Odie is a mixed breed. His mother was a beagle and
his father was a brick!

Where's the best place to buy a dog like Odie?
At the pest shop!

What did Odie say when he sat on the sandpaper?
"Ruff!"

What is Odie's favorite movie snack?
A big box of pupcorn!

What pet does Odie always trip over?
The *car*pet.

Why was Odie chasing the marching band?
He wanted to bury the trombones!

Odie left his brain to science ... and it looks like they
made an early withdrawal!

"If I had a dog like Odie and you had a dog like Odie,
what would we have?"
"Too many dogs like Odie!"

When is Odie like a door?
When Garfield slams him!

What did Jon say when Odie left the room?
"Doggone."

Why was Odie standing on the chair?
He was trying to raise his I.Q.

Where should Odie look if he wants a good scare?
In the mirror!

What would you get if you crossed Odie with a palm tree?
A dog who's coconuts!

What is Odie's favorite baseball team?
The New York Mutts.

Odie's breath is so bad, his reflection has to wear a gas mask!

What would you call it if Odie's face fell off?
An improvement!

What was Odie doing in the clothes dryer?
About forty revolutions per minute!

You have to expect Odie to be clumsy. After all, he has two left paws!

I'm not saying that Odie is dumb, but he once tried to fish off the back of a rowing machine!

Is Odie a watchdog?
Yes. If burglars break in, Odie watches them take everything.

How did Odie win his fight with Garfield?
He got in a few good licks!

How did Jon make Odie smell better?
He had him de*odie*rized!

What was Odie doing in front of the microwave?
Waiting for someone to change the channel.

TOP TEN ADVANTAGES
TO BEING ODIE

10. Never has to write a book report
 9. Plenty of saliva for throwing spitballs
 8. Isn't flustered if he forgets to give "Jeopardy" answer in the form of a question
 7. Bathroom always as close as the nearest tree

6. Tongue can reach those "hard-to-lick" places
5. Babes dig cartoon characters
4. Okay to scratch himself in public
3. Can't insult his intelligence; he doesn't have any!
2. Gets to drink from his own private toilet
1. He's naked all the time!

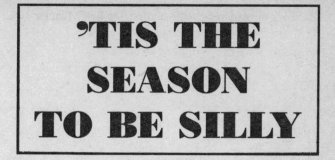

'TIS THE SEASON TO BE SILLY

So many necks, so little time

What is Garfield's favorite type of Halloween candy?
Lotsa candy.

Why is Odie like a jack-o'-lantern?
They both have empty heads.

Know why graveyards have fences around them?
Because people are dying to get in!

Where do spooks go to mail a letter?
The ghost office.

What's orange and black and has a bolt in its neck?
Garfieldstein.

What did the vampire say to the Invisible Man?
"Long time, no see!"

When is it bad luck to have a black cat follow you?
When you're a mouse!

Knock knock!
Who's there?
Witch.
Witch who?
Witch you'd stop asking questions and let me in!

What happened when the little witch misbehaved?
She was sent to her broom.

What do you call a ghost who styles your hair?
A bootician!

What did the polite vampire say to his victim?
"It's been nice gnawing you!"

What do you say to a depressed vampire?
"Fang in there!"

How do you make a skeleton laugh?
Try tickling his funny bone!

What would you get if you crossed Halloween with
Christmas?
A ghoul Yule!

What is Dracula's favorite line for meeting girls?
"Hey, gorgeous. What's your blood type?"

How come vampires never seem to have any friends?
Because they're a pain in the neck!

How did the ghost look in her designer sheet?
Boo-tiful!

What did the angry skeleton say to the other skeleton?
"I have a bone to pick with you!"

What do little spooks call their parents?
Mummy and Deady.

Why was Frankenstein acting so strangely?
His head wasn't screwed on right.

Where do little monsters play at recess?
In the ghoulyard!

Why do people seem so tired on April Fools' Day?
Because they've just had a long March!

What is a dog's favorite Easter treat?
Jelly bones!

What has big ears, brings Easter treats, and goes
    hippity-BOOM, hippity-BOOM, hippity-BOOM?
The Easter Elephant.

How does the Easter Bunny stay in shape?
He does lots of hare-obics.

Why didn't Garfield eat his chocolate bunnies right
    away?
He was waiting for them to multiply!

How should you send a letter to the Easter Bunny?
By hare mail!

Knock knock!
Who's there?
Philip.
Philip who?
Philip my basket with candy!

What has long ears, brings treats, and leaves a mess
    on your carpet?
The Easter Odie.

What do you need if your chocolate eggs mysteriously
    disappear?
You need an eggsplanation!

How did the soggy Easter Bunny dry himself?
With a hare dryer!

How is the Easter Bunny like Michael Jordan?
They're both famous for stuffing baskets!

What's red and blue and sogs up your Easter basket?
Colored scrambled eggs!

What's the best way to stuff a turkey?
Serve him lots of pizza and ice cream!

If April showers bring May flowers, what do May
     flowers bring?
Pilgrims!

Why did the Pilgrims eat turkey at Thanksgiving?
Because they couldn't get the moose in the oven!

What did the turkey say to the turkey hunter?
"Quack! Quack! Quack!"

What's big and purple and floats over the Macy's
     parade?
A hot-air grape.

What did the Pilgrim vampire celebrate?
Fangsgiving!

Knock knock!
Who's there?
Earl.
Earl who?
Earl I want for Christmas is lots of everything!

Why does Santa use reindeer to pull his sleigh?
Because the elephants kept crashing through the roof!

Why did Odie fetch Jon's hedge clippers on Christmas
Eve?
Because he heard Jon say it was time to trim the tree.

What would you get if you crossed a pig with a
Christmas tree?
A porker pine!

What is Tarzan's favorite Christmas carol?
"Jungle Bells."

Knock Knock!
Who's there?
Doc.
Doc who?
Doc the halls with boughs of holly!

Why is Santa like a busy gardener?
Because all he does is hoe, hoe, hoe!

What would you get if you crossed Santa Claus with
Garfield?
A jolly old elf who fills your stocking and empties your
fridge!

GARFIELD'S TOP TEN THINGS TO DO ON CHRISTMAS EVE

10. Heckle carolers
 9. Roast pizza on an open fire
 8. Enlarge stocking
 7. Test mistletoe. Often
 6. Get nog-faced
 5. Take long winter's nap
 4. Start Christmas shopping
 3. Fax last-minute demands to North Pole
 2. Fake being good one more time
 1. Bait the Santa trap

JEST FOR FUN

I know you're out there.
I can hear your lips moving

Why did the girl wear loud socks?
To keep her feet from falling asleep!

Why did the woman put a clock under her desk?
She wanted to work overtime.

Why is Jon Arbuckle like a faulty calendar?
They both have a lot of bad dates!

"Did you hear about Pete? He fell off a fifty-foot ladder
    and didn't get hurt."
"That's a miracle!"
"Not really. He fell off the bottom rung."

Why does a man who has just shaved look like Pooky?
Because he has a bare face.

"Are those bunny slippers comfortable?"
"I'll say. It's like walking on hare!"

Jon is such a wimp, he gets seasick in the bathtub!

Why is it so wet in England?
Because there's always a king or queen reigning there.

Why are dolphins so smart?
Because they live in schools.

Why did the man buy an elephant instead of a car?
The elephant had a bigger trunk.

Then there was the runner who wanted to run faster,
    so he filled his shoes with quicksand.

Teacher: "Why do hummingbirds hum?"
Student: "Maybe they forgot the words!"

"How did you sleep last night?"
"With my eyes closed, of course!"

"What's the best way to keep water from coming into
    my house?"
"Don't pay your water bill!"

"Did you take a bath?"
"Why? Is there one missing?"

What kind of shellfish makes you stronger?
Mussels.

Why do frogs make lousy pets?
Because they always croak.

Why did the man keep his money in the refrigerator?
He liked cold cash.

"How was your ride on the roller coaster?"
"It had its ups and downs."

What has two feet, two tongues, and lots of eyes?
A pair of shoes.

Did you hear about the new movie starring a dachshund?
It sounds like a real wiener!

Then there was the lady who was such a lousy
gardener, even her artificial plants died!

Teacher: "What word do people always pronounce
wrong?"
Student: "Wrong."

What's the best day to go to the beach?
*Sun*day, of course!

Cop: "Have you ever been arrested?"
Suspect: "Yes. After my nap, I'm always arrested."

Mom: "I want you to straighten up your room."
Son: "Why? Is it crooked?"

"The guys won't let me join their club. What should I do?"
"Get your own club and hit them with it!"

Teacher: "Where was the Declaration of Independence signed?"
Student: "On the bottom!"

What's stinky and goes two hundred miles per hour?
Jon's sweatsocks in a blender!

What did the carpenter say to the board?
"I'll be sawing you."

What did the flower say to the bee?
"Buzz off!"

Why did Sir Lancelot sleep during the day?
Because he was on the knight shift.

"Do you like doing aerobics with dumbbells?"
"It's okay. But I prefer smart people."

Which of the Great lakes is the spookiest?
Lake Eerie.

Then there was the guy who was so dumb, he went to
a garage sale to buy a garage.

Knock knock!
Who's there?
Ken.
Ken who?
Ken you come out and play?

"What would you say to a hot dog?"
"I'd tell him to go inside and cool off!"

"I call my cat 'Boomerang.' "
"Why is that?"
"Because I throw him out, but he always comes back!"

When does a mouse weigh as much as an elephant?
When the scale is broken.

Why doesn't Odie use toothpaste?
None of his teeth are loose!

Why is February like "Forward"?
They both come before March!

Bunny 1: "Can you give me two more carrots? I need
   them to cure my sniffles."
Bunny 2: "But you've already eaten a dozen."
Bunny 1: "I know. But this is a genuine fourteen-carrot
   cold."

"If you ever need a brain transplant, get one from a
   dog."
"Why would I want a dog brain?"
"Because you can be certain that it's never been
   used!"

What did the teapot say to the stove?
"You get me all steamed up!"

What's orange and black and blue all over?
Garfield in the freezer.

Then there was the dog who was so lazy, he only chased parked cars!

Cat 1: "This dog named Spot keeps following me. How can I get rid of him?"
Cat 2: "Have you tried spot remover?"

TOP TEN TOYS
FOR DELINQUENT CATS

10. "Buffy, the Inflatable Love Kitten"
 9. Studded-leather scratching post
 8. Officer McGruff punching bag
 7. Tiny brass knuckles
 6. Yarn noose
 5. Stiletto with can-opener attachment
 4. Birdzooka
 3. Ball of piano wire
 2. "Bag o' Frightened Middle-Class Mice"
 1. Puppy on a string

PARTY ON!

Let's get cake-faced!

Why do karate experts wear black belts?

Why was Odie standing on his head at the birthday
    party?
He heard they were having upside-down cake!

When is a birthday cake like a golf ball?
When it's been sliced.

Knock knock!
Who's there?
Gus.
Gus who?
Gus how old I am today!

"Why are you cutting the cake with a chisel?"
"Because it's marble cake."

How did the dumb dog know it was his birthday?
He didn't. The cat had to remind him.

Knock knock!
Who's there?
Ivan.
Ivan who?
Ivan a piece of your cake!

How can you tell when Garfield's birthday party is
    over?
The riot police go home.

Knock knock!
Who's there?
Freddy.
Freddy who?
Freddy to open your presents?

Why did the man act wild and crazy on his birthday?
He was trying to age disgracefully!

For his birthday Jon asked for a heavy sweater. So
    Garfield gave him a sumo wrestler!

What does Garfield always get on his birthday?
Another year older.

Why did the man put the cake in the freezer?
Because his wife said it was time to ice it.

Knock knock!
Who's there?
Ben.
Ben who?
Ben over and get your birthday spanking!

Why does Garfield take extra naps on June 19?
Because he likes to have a nappy birthday!

What's the difference between a dog and a birthday
    candle?
The candle is about a thousand times brighter!

Knock knock!
Who's there?
Omar.
Omar who?
Omar goodness! Your present escaped!

"Were any famous men or women born on your birthday?"
"No, only little babies."

Why do we put candles on top of a birthday cake?
Because it's too hard to put them on the bottom.

What kind of birthday did the frog have?
A hoppy one!

"Ugh! There's a fish in this envelope!"
"Guess someone sent you a birthday cod!"

Knock knock!
Who's there?
Abby and Minnie.
Abby and Minnie who?
Abby Birthday and Minnie Happy Returns!

What is Garfield's favorite party game?
"Pin the Nermal on the Donkey."

How can you tell when your cake has too many candles?
When the fire department has to hose it out!

Then there was the guy who partied till the cows came home ... and then he partied with the cows!

Why did the rabbit run off with the birthday cake?
It was carrot cake!

Duchess: "What shall we give the king for his birthday?"
Duke: "How about some birthday peasants?"

What kind of party should you have when you get new tires for your car?
A re*tire*ment party!

How can you tell a well-dressed party animal?
His socks match the lampshade he's wearing.

Why do party animals always wear pants with pockets?
So they have some place to keep their bail money.

Why didn't the cow go to the party?
She wasn't in the moo-d.

Why do party animals usually sit on the floor?
So they won't have so far to fall.

Teacher: "Why does our country have a two-party system?"
Student: "So we can have one party on Friday and one on Saturday!"

Why did the teenager take a sledgehammer to the party?
Because he heard it was going to be a big bash!

"When is your birthday?"
"August 26."
"What year?"
"Every year!"

Knock knock!
Who's there?
Matty.
Matty who?
Matty nice of you to invite me to the party!

TOP TEN THINGS GARFIELD WOULD LIKE FOR HIS BIRTHDAY

10. Nermal deported
9. Pet goldfish, with a side order of fries
8. Combination back scratcher–spider whacker
7. Diving board for his food dish
6. Giant autographed poster of himself
5. Bird grater
4. Muzzle for Jon
3. Electric doggy prod
2. New cat bed with Italian restaurant attached
1. Party with 10,000 of his closest, gift-bearing friends

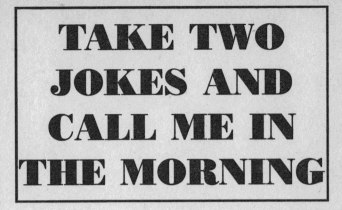

TAKE TWO JOKES AND CALL ME IN THE MORNING

Medicine is a sick business

"Mr. Johnson, you are very sick."
"Doctor, I want a second opinion."
"Okay. You're also ugly."

"Doctor, how can I avoid feeling run down?"
"Look both ways before you cross the street."

"Doctor, whenever I drink coffee, I get a sharp pain in
    my eye."
"Try taking the spoon out of the cup."

"Doctor, my wife keeps complaining about my
    snoring."
"Is it loud?"
"Oh, yes, she really screams."

"Doctor, I have this nagging pain."
"Where is it?"
"She's at home right now."

"Doctor, I have a pain in my liver."
"How do you know it's your liver?"
"Well, if it's not mine, whose would it be?"

"Doctor, my brother thinks he's a dog."
"That's a real problem."
"I know. Our apartment doesn't allow pets."

"Doctor, can you fix a hernia?"
"Yes."
"I'll be back after I move the piano."

"Doctor, I think I'm losing my memory."
"How long have you had this problem?"
"What problem?"

"Mr. Smith, you're suffering from low blood pressure."
"How can I raise it, Doctor?"
"Here. Take a look at your bill."

120

"Doctor, my nose keeps growing. It's twelve inches long!"

"Then you'd better see a foot doctor."

"Doctor, there's something hairy growing out of my neck."

"That's your head."

"Doctor, what can I do about my insomnia?"

"If I were you, I'd sleep on it."

"I have good news and bad news, Mr. Smith. The bad news is, you need a very expensive operation."

"What's the good news, Doctor?"

"Now I can afford that new Mercedes!"

"Doctor, I have a back problem."

"It looks more like you've been in a fight."

"That's what I mean: I hit some guy, and he hit me back."

"Doctor, my stomach hurts after I eat lunch."

"Do you have ulcers?"

"No, just a sandwich and fries."

"Doctor, can you remove an unsightly blemish?"
"I suppose."
"Good. I want you to get rid of my sister."

"Doctor, my face is killing me."
"It's not making *me* feel too good, either."

"Doctor, will this shot hurt?"
"Not a bit."
"Ouch! You said it wouldn't hurt a bit."
"And it didn't. It hurt a lot."

"Doctor, I accidentally drank my dog's medicine. Will it affect me?"
"I doubt it. Now sit up and give me your paw."

"How did you hurt your head, Mr. Jones?"
"I kissed a girl."
"Kissing doesn't cause a lump like that."
"It does if your wife walks in."

"Doctor, do you make house calls?"
"Yes, I do."
"Then call my house and tell my wife to hold dinner."

122

"Doctor, what would you say if I told you I had a brain tumor?"
"I'd say it was all in your head."

"Doctor, do you give discounts to senior citizens?"
"Yes."
"Then I'll come back in thirty years."

"Tommy, I'm going to take your pulse."
"All right, Doctor. But be sure to give it back."

"I think surgeons must be the funniest doctors."
"Why is that?"
"They always leave their patients in stitches!"

"My mom took my new sister to the doctor."
"Is he a baby doctor?"
"No, he's all grown up."

"Doctor, can you help me? I sleep like a baby."
"But that's good."
"No, I wake up every hour and cry!"

"My crazy uncle has been seeing ghosts."
"He should see a psychiatrist."
"Why? The ghosts are cheaper."

"How is your eyesight, Mr. Wilson?"
"Failing, Doctor. I can barely see my wife."
"That's sad."
"You haven't seen my wife."

"My five-year-old is going to be a great doctor."
"How can you tell?"
"He already knows how to make us wait."

TOP TEN SIGNS THAT YOU'VE GONE TO A BAD VETERINARIAN

10. Moonlights as a taxidermist
 9. Keeps excusing himself to check the traps
 8. Disgruntled buffaloes are picketing outside his office
 7. Can't work a "pooper scooper"
 6. Introduces himself as Dr. Rogers, smiles, then asks, "Can you say *neutered*?"
 5. Only licensed to treat invertebrates
 4. Two words: power tools
 3. Refuses to call a spayed a spayed
 2. Keeps confusing Mr. Ed with Mr. T
 1. He's wearing a poochskin cap

LAST LAUGHS

*It's hard to be serious
when you're naked*

Why did the man run around his bed?
He was trying to catch up on his sleep.

What did the hunter say after a week in the jungle?
"Safari, so good!"

What's black, wrinkled, and thunders across the
plains?
A herd of raisins.

What's the worst kind of tile to put on your kitchen
floor?
A reptile!

What kind of dress does every girl have, but never
wear?
An ad-dress!

Why does Nermal read adventure stories?
Because kittens love a good yarn!

How many dieters does it take to eat a sundae?
Five. One to eat the sundae and four to share the guilt.

Then there was the dieter who was so skinny, every
time he went out, someone tried to fly a flag from
him!

"Waiter, this coffee tastes like mud!"
"Of course. It was ground this morning."

How do you drive an inchworm crazy?
Make him convert to the metric system!

Why is it dangerous for skinny people to jog?
They keep falling through the cracks in the sidewalk.

What do skinny people do for fun?
They like to count their ribs.

Knock knock!
Who's there?
Frank Lee.
Frank Lee who?
Frank Lee, that's none of your business!

Why did the teenager put his boombox in the oven?
He wanted to hear some hot tunes.

Why did the camper tiptoe through the camp?
He didn't want to wake the sleeping bags.

Why did the man take a clock on the airplane?
He wanted to make time fly.

How did the scientist communicate with the fish?
He dropped them a line.

How did Garfield swallow an entire room?
It was a *mush*-room.

Why did the girl put sugar on her pillow?
She wanted to have sweet dreams.

What's the best way to catch a rabbit?
Hide in the bushes and make a noise like a carrot.

What do you call a dieter who gains weight?
Cured!

Why is it smart to take skinny people along when you
go camping?
You can always rub two of them together to start a
fire.

Why did the boy take his piggy bank outside?
He heard there was going to be some change in the
weather.

What does an 800-lb. parrot say?
"Polly wants a cracker NOW!"

Why did the boy make a guitar out of iron?
So he could play heavy-metal music!

What's the difference between a skinny person and a stick?
A stick doesn't complain when a dog fetches it.

Knock knock!
Who's there?
Wanda.
Wanda who?
Wanda drop by to say "hi!"

What did the big flower say to the little flower?
"Hi, Bud!"

Zookeeper 1: "That little chimp acts just like his father."
Zookeeper 2: "Yes, he's a regular chimp off the old block."

Teacher: "Why do the cows eat green grass?"
Student: "Because they can't wait for it to get ripe!"

What's heavier in summer than in winter?
Traffic to the beach!

Why do karate experts wear black belts?
To keep their pants from falling down!

Hunter 1: "Have you ever hunted bear?"
Hunter 2: "No, but I've camped out in my underwear."

Did you hear about the basketball player who couldn't
    make a basket?
He was a hoopless case!

Why did the dolphin see a guidance counselor?
He wanted to find his porpoise in life.

What animal talks all the time?
A yak.

What would you get if you crossed Pooky with Arnold
    Schwarzenegger?
A cuddly bear who says, "Sleep tight ... or I rip your
    lungs out."

How did the undertaker speak?
Gravely.

"Do my clothes make a statement?"
"Yes. The statement is: 'I have no taste!' "

TOP TEN INCORRECT WAYS OF SAYING
"BIG FAT HAIRY DEAL"

10. "Big fat hairy duck"
 9. "Big fat dickory dock"
 8. "Land o' goshen"
 7. "Big fit happy seal"
 6. "Big fat ferris wheel"
 5. "Large obese hirsute agreement"
 4. "Makes me no nevermind"
 3. "Big fat cherry peel"
 2. "Big fat furry veal"
 1. "So what?"

"Knock knock!"
"Who's there?"
"Noah."
"Noah who?"
"Noah more jokes, please!"

GARFIELD
and the gang
are available at bookstores everywhere.
Published by Ballantine Books.

Call toll free 1-800-733-3000 to order by phone and use your major credit card. Or use this coupon to order by mail.

__GARFIELD AT LARGE	32013-1	$6.95
__GARFIELD GAINS WEIGHT	32008-5	$6.95
__GARFIELD BIGGER THAN LIFE	32007-7	$6.95
__GARFIELD WEIGHS IN	32010-7	$6.95
__GARFIELD TAKES THE CAKE	32009-3	$6.95
__GARFIELD EATS HIS HEART OUT	32018-2	$6.95
__GARFIELD SITS AROUND THE HOUSE	32011-5	$6.95
__GARFIELD TIPS THE SCALES	33580-5	$6.95
__GARFIELD LOSES HIS FEET	31805-6	$6.95
__GARFIELD MAKES IT BIG	31928-1	$6.95
__GARFIELD ROLLS ON	32634-2	$6.95
__GARFIELD OUT TO LUNCH	33118-4	$6.95
__GARFIELD FOOD FOR THOUGHT	34129-5	$6.95
__GARFIELD SWALLOWS HIS PRIDE	34725-0	$6.95
__GARFIELD WORLDWIDE	35158-4	$6.95
__GARFIELD ROUNDS OUT	35388-9	$6.95
__GARFIELD CHEWS THE FAT	35956-9	$6.95
__GARFIELD GOES TO WAIST	36430-9	$6.95
__GARFIELD HANGS OUT	36835-5	$6.95
__GARFIELD TAKES UP SPACE	37029-5	$6.95
__GARFIELD BY THE POUND	37579-3	$6.95
__GARFIELD SAYS A MOUTHFUL	37368-5	$6.95
__GARFIELD KEEPS HIS CHINS	37959-4	$6.95
__GARFIELD TAKES HIS LICKS	38170-X	$6.95
__GARFIELD HITS THE BIG TIME	38332-X	$6.95

Name_____

Address_____

City_____State_____Zip_____

Please send me the BALLANTINE BOOKS I have checked above.

I am enclosing	$_____
plus	
Postage & handling*	$_____
Sales tax (where applicable)	$_____
Total amount enclosed	$_____

*Add $2 for the first book and 50¢ for each additional book.

Send check or money order (no cash or CODs) to:
Ballantine Mail Sales, 400 Hahn Road, Westminster, MD 21157.

Prices and numbers subject to change without notice.
Valid in the U.S. only.
All orders subject to availability.   DAVIS